FRANNIE MEISEN

How To Interview People

Hire the Perfect Person Every Time

Copyright © 2024 by Frannie Meisen

All rights reserved. No part of this publication may be reproduced, stored or transmitted in any form or by any means, electronic, mechanical, photocopying, recording, scanning, or otherwise without written permission from the publisher. It is illegal to copy this book, post it to a website, or distribute it by any other means without permission.

Frannie Meisen asserts the moral right to be identified as the author of this work.

Frannie Meisen has no responsibility for the persistence or accuracy of URLs for external or third-party Internet Websites referred to in this publication and does not guarantee that any content on such Websites is, or will remain, accurate or appropriate.

Designations used by companies to distinguish their products are often claimed as trademarks. All brand names and product names used in this book and on its cover are trade names, service marks, trademarks and registered trademarks of their respective owners. The publishers and the book are not associated with any product or vendor mentioned in this book. None of the companies referenced within the book have endorsed the book.

First edition

This book was professionally typeset on Reedsy.
Find out more at reedsy.com

For A. and B., with Deepest Gratitude

Contents

1. INTRODUCTION — 1
   Why I Wrote This Book — 1
2. CHAPTER 1 — 5
   Getting Clear on What You Need: Credentials and Chemistry — 5
3. CHAPTER 2 — 10
   After the Resumé, Before the Interview — 10
4. CHAPTER 3 — 15
   Creating a Comfortable and Open Interview Environment — 15
5. CHAPTER 4 — 19
   The Interview Template — 19
6. CONCLUSION — 34
7. Resources — 37

1

INTRODUCTION

Why I Wrote This Book

Interviewing is both a skill and an art. While anyone can review qualifications and professional backgrounds, uncovering the true person behind the resumé requires a deeper approach. This book is designed to provide you with a blueprint for successful interviewing in any scenario, as well as a clear understanding of the thought process behind it. In the following chapters, I will discuss the two primary components that must be explored in any interview for hiring success, as well as share my personal interview template that reliably yields solid insights into my job candidates every time.

Personally, I love interviewing people. It is an intuitive process that I enjoy. My career as an Executive Recruiter provided me with the opportunity to hone this skill set and create the methodology laid out in this book. However, there are other things I learned during my time in recruitment as well.

The modern workplace has become increasingly isolated,

relying on remote or hybrid setups. The hiring process has followed suit. It is now not uncommon for an entire interview process to occur virtually, with the candidate stepping into the office for the first time on their first day of work (if there even is a centralized workplace). This lack of personal interaction presents specific challenges for interviewing. Currently, what is most often meant by a "face-to-face" interview is one that takes place via video. While this is far better than a phone call, it is not the same as being able to meet someone in person, reading their body language and overall energy. Given these realities, it has never been more important to get the process of interviewing right.

The ability to both be interviewed as well as conduct one are essential skills. It became apparent to me that young professionals in the earlier stages of their careers lack a clear understanding of how to best perform on either side of the interview process. While there are likely many reasons for this, the reality is that hiring and retention rates will suffer in the absence of a thorough, trained interview process conducted by well-trained employees.

In researching this book, I discovered that plenty has been written to support the job candidate on how to interview effectively. But what about the person conducting the interview? I was surprised to see how little coverage there was on this topic. I decided to write this book in the hopes that it can be of use to anyone undertaking a hiring process.

INTRODUCTION

Who Is This Book For?

The answer is simple: everyone.

This might surprise you given your current situation. You may not be working full-time in an office setting, or you might not be in human resources, recruiting, or any professional hiring capacity for that matter. However, you will likely need to interview people for important roles at some point in your life. Whether hiring a caregiver for your children or aging parents, looking for a house sitter, a tutor, or a personal assistant, it is crucial to go into the interview knowing exactly what you need and how to determine if the person you're interviewing fits that need, and most importantly, if they are the right fit for your environment.

What Is Covered in This Book

This book covers all aspects of conducting a face-to-face interview, whether the interview takes place online via video meeting or in person. This book is designed to provide guidance on conducting a substantial, early stage interview after an initial screening call but before later stage discussions, the success of which depends, at least in part, on an effective and thorough first round interview. While a conversation over the phone is an acceptable first step in the screening process, all interactions from that point on should be face-to-face, virtual or in person. A phone conversation does not allow you, the interviewer, to read visual cues or body language, both of which are essential for conducting an effective and successful interview.

You will learn the nuances of creating a comfortable and open environment where candidates feel at ease to express themselves authentically. The book provides detailed strategies on how to ask probing questions that reveal the true capabilities and potential of the candidate. You'll also gain insights into interpreting non-verbal cues and understanding the subtle dynamics of communication that go beyond spoken words.

Additionally, this book addresses the challenges and opportunities of conducting virtual interviews. It offers practical advice on setting up a professional virtual environment, ensuring technical reliability, and maintaining the human touch in digital interactions. The goal is to equip you with the skills to navigate the complexities of modern interviewing, ensuring you can effectively assess candidates regardless of the medium.

By the end of this book, you will have a comprehensive toolkit for conducting thorough, enjoyable, and effective "in-person" interviews, regardless of the role. You will be able to approach each interview with confidence, knowing that you have the knowledge and skills to identify the best candidates for any position.

2

CHAPTER 1

Getting Clear on What You Need: Credentials and Chemistry

Knowing what you need is a vital part of any hiring process. If you are working from a job description, then you have already clarified the requirements of the role and the necessary skill set(s). However, reduced staffing and shorter timelines often result in a "tick the boxes" mentality, working from a checklist that only covers the most basic aspects of the open role. A candidate is eventually identified and hired, with everyone hoping that the hire was successful and will last at the company.

Let me ask you this: What are you really looking for? The answer might appear obvious, as in "We need a new assistant for our CEO." Yes, you do need a new assistant for the CEO. But how long do you want them to stay in the role and at your company? This perspective is often overlooked in the hiring process, yet it can make all the difference in making a great hire. Whether or not the person stays on and becomes an integral member of your company is often thought of as something you have no control over. You simply hope that it will all work out and you won't be hiring for this role again within the next two years.

Interviewing for longevity requires us to dig deeper. You are not looking simply to fill the role; you're bringing someone new into a community that has its own culture, values, and customs. Not only do you need to confirm that your candidate has the professional experience required for the role, but you also have to assess them for "fit" and make a judgment call as to whether or not they are the right choice for your company.

You might be thinking, "That all makes sense, but how do I do that?" The answer can be distilled down to two essential factors: Credentials and Chemistry.

Credentials

Taken at face value, "credentials" is the more obvious component to screen for. Credentials clearly refer to the stated experience and skills listed on a candidate's resumé, and this is where to start your selection process. Do they have the required years of experience in your field? Do they meet your basic requirements for education? Have they listed any professional achievements that you would like them to carry over in the role at your company? Their stated experience is a jumping-off point for a more in-depth discussion of their background, experience, accomplishments, and ambition for the future. The upcoming interview will be an opportunity for you to evaluate their experience and determine if it meets the needs of your open position.

To further delve into their credentials, consider these strategies:

- **Behavioral Questions**: Ask candidates to describe past experiences where they demonstrated key skills. For example, "Can you tell me about a time when you had to manage a challenging project under tight deadlines?"
- **Scenario-Based Questions**: Pose hypothetical situations relevant to the role and assess how they would handle them. For example, "How would you approach a situation where you had to mediate a conflict between team members?"

Chemistry

Chemistry is the more elusive of these two components, but it is no less important than credentials. In fact, my experience is that often it is more so. Let's say you hired someone with terrific credentials who answered your questions well enough in the interview process. Shortly after starting the job, it becomes clear that they don't fit in with your team or cannot establish a rapport with their supervisor. It's only a matter of time before that employee leaves or is let go, and you're back to square one.

What is chemistry in this context anyway? Personality and social abilities factor into the definition, but in the end, chemistry is all about connection. It's a primary driver in all social relationships—family, friends, and romantic partners. It's no different when considering if someone is a good fit for your open role. That role is part of a larger network (your workplace) with its own distinct energy. It's essential to go into the interview process with a clear picture of what social and behavioral traits your candidate needs to embody in order to be successful.

To effectively evaluate chemistry, consider these approaches:

- **Cultural Fit Questions:** Ask about their preferred work environment, values, and how they handle teamwork. For instance, "Can you describe the type of work environment where you feel most productive and happy?"
- **Team Interaction:** If possible, involve potential team members in the interview process to see how well the candidate interacts with them.

Credentials vs. Chemistry: A Delicate Balance

Is one of these components more important than the other? While it is essential to screen for both chemistry and credentials in all cases, the extent to which one is more important than the other depends on several factors.

For instance, it's easy to assume that if a role is remote, then it's acceptable for the new hire to be naturally shy, more comfortable working at home in a quiet environment. However, are there regular meetings with colleagues online? Is a lot of daily conversation required with that person's supervisor? While your workforce may not consistently be in one place at the same time, it's still important to screen for fit with your company culture and team energy, in other words, for chemistry.

Every interview needs to contain prompts designed to gain a deeper understanding of the candidate in each of these areas.

CHAPTER 1

Tailor your questions to uncover insights about both their professional abilities and their potential to integrate seamlessly with your team. This holistic approach ensures that you are not only hiring someone who can do the job but someone who will thrive in your unique work environment, contributing positively to the overall culture and success of your organization.

By focusing on both credentials and chemistry, you will be well-equipped to make hiring decisions that are not only effective in the short term but sustainable in the long run, ensuring the growth and stability of your team.

CHAPTER 2

After the Resumé, Before the Interview

There are several steps you can take to gain a deeper understanding of your candidates before your initial meeting with them. The following suggestions may not be news to experienced hiring professionals. For others, these are good ways to begin to get a more complete picture of your candidate before you have ever spoken with them.

The most obvious place to start is with your candidate's online presence. There are several websites to review, and your company most likely has a protocol regarding the online visibility of potential employees; we won't go into that here. For our purposes, the site to discuss is LinkedIn.

LinkedIn

LinkedIn is the leading networking site for business professionals and has therefore become an essential tool in today's marketplace. Anyone actively engaged in a job search should have an up-to-date and complete LinkedIn profile. There are four main things to look for in any profile that will give you a deeper understanding of your candidates.

Posts

This is an obvious place to start looking further into your candidates. What are they posting, and how is it being received? How many reposts or reactions are their posts getting? While this is a great starting point, the other profile components will provide further insight than reviewing posts alone.

Profile Completion

A strong candidate will have a complete and up-to-date profile with a downloadable resumé and a profile picture. This indicates that they are serious about finding a job and understand the importance of being visible on the site. Look for detailed descriptions of their roles, accomplishments, and skills, as these reflect their professionalism and commitment to showcasing their expertise.

Connections

Take a look at the number of connections they have. This is an important indicator of how engaged they are in networking in their area and/or industry. If you are interviewing for a high-touch role in an area such as human resources, you will want to see several hundred connections on the site. LinkedIn will show the exact number of connections up to 499. Anything over 500 is listed as "500+." Seeing that "500+" is another strong indicator that they are engaged professionals, something you most likely want on your team.

Next, have a look at who those connections are. Are they in your industry? In your company? Or, are the majority of connections conspicuously outside of their professional experience? I once had a candidate who had more than 500+ connections, but when I looked more closely at who he was following and who the connections were, they were almost all musicians or affiliated with the music industry, entirely outside his own professional experience to date and having nothing to do with the job he had applied for with me. While this was not a reason to reject the candidate outright, it did caution me as to how serious he might be about our industry and the role. Not surprisingly, he did not stack up to the other candidates we interviewed for that position.

Chapter 2

Following

Who is your candidate following? Are they following companies or thought leaders in your industry? If they have applied to your role and/or have had a preliminary screening conversation, they should have started following your company. This demonstrates a proactive interest and engagement with your industry and organization, indicating they are serious about the opportunity.

Resumé Review (One More Time)

Depending on the specifics of the role you need to fill, the pressure to hire, and the available candidate pool, you may have selected a few resumés that don't meet your usual high standards. Sometimes a decision is made to interview a candidate based on their experience despite a less-than-stellar resumé. Perhaps there are a few inconsistencies that you have decided to live with. What is the nature of those mistakes? Grammatical errors? Inconsistencies in the formatting or font? Could the information be more clearly presented? Is the information hard to read or understand?

It's counter intuitive to say that you want to find a typo or inconsistency on a resumé. However, such missteps present you as the interviewer with a great opportunity to find out how your candidate responds to constructive criticism.

I would often say to a candidate, "Are you open to feedback on your resumé?" Even if the response was favorable, it was easy to tell if they were truly open to criticism, which is a quality I'd like to see in anyone worthy of hiring. This approach helps you assess their willingness to learn, their attention to detail, and their ability to handle feedback—a crucial indicator of the likelihood for professional growth and collaboration.

In addition to these steps, consider implementing the following strategies to gain further insights:

- **Pre-Interview Questionnaire:** Send a short questionnaire to candidates before the interview. Include questions about their motivations, career goals, and expectations for the role. This can provide valuable context and help you tailor your interview questions.
- **Reference Checks:** Reach out to the provided references to get a sense of the candidate's work ethic, personality, and compatibility with your company culture. Asking specific questions about their strengths and areas for improvement can reveal critical insights.
- **Skill Assessments:** Depending on the role, consider administering skill assessments or tests relevant to the job. This can give you a more objective measure of their capabilities and help you compare candidates more effectively.

By thoroughly reviewing a candidate's online presence, engaging with their resumé critically, and utilizing additional assessment tools, you can build a comprehensive understanding of who they are before the interview. This preparation sets the stage for a more productive and insightful conversation, ultimately leading to better hiring decisions.

4

CHAPTER 3

Creating a Comfortable and Open Interview Environment

In the highly charged world of interviewing, the atmosphere you create can make or break the process. A comfortable and open environment allows candidates to express themselves authentically, providing you with the most accurate representation of their capabilities and potential. This chapter will delve into the nuances of building such an environment and offer detailed strategies to help you master this crucial aspect of interviewing.

Setting the Stage

The physical setting of the interview plays a significant role in how comfortable a candidate feels. Whether the interview is conducted in person or virtually, it is equally important to ensure the space is welcoming, professional, and free of distractions.

In-Person Interviews:

- **Location:** Choose a quiet, well-lit room with comfortable seating. Avoid cramped spaces that can make candidates feel confined.
- **Setup:** Arrange the seating to promote a conversational tone. Sitting across a desk can feel formal and intimidating; instead, consider sitting at a round table or in a more casual seating arrangement.
- **Details:** Small touches like offering water or coffee and ensuring the room is at a comfortable temperature can make a big difference in putting candidates at ease.

Virtual Interviews:

- **Technical Setup:** Ensure a stable internet connection, good lighting, and clear audio. Test your equipment beforehand to avoid technical glitches that can disrupt the flow of the interview.
- **Background:** Choose a neutral, uncluttered background that reflects a professional image. Virtual backgrounds should be used sparingly, as they can sometimes be distracting. Blurring your background is a great option.
- Presence: Maintain eye contact by looking at the camera, not the screen. This helps create a sense of connection despite the physical distance.

CHAPTER 3

Conducting Virtual Interviews

The rise of remote work has made virtual interviews a common practice. While they offer convenience, they also present unique challenges that require careful management to ensure a productive and insightful interview.

Practical Tips for Virtual Interviews:

- **Professional Environment:** Just as with in-person interviews, ensure that your virtual environment is professional and free of distractions.
- **Technical Reliability:** Test your equipment and internet connection beforehand. Have a backup plan in case of technical issues.
- **Human Touch:** Make an extra effort to connect with the candidate. Use their name frequently, maintain eye contact, and be mindful of your tone and body language to convey warmth and engagement.

Navigating the Complexities of Modern Interviewing

Modern interviewing involves a blend of in-person and virtual techniques, each with its own set of complexities. To effectively assess candidates regardless of the medium, it's crucial to be adaptable and prepared for any scenario.

In-Person vs. Virtual Interviews:

- **Consistency:** Ensure that your assessment criteria are consistent across both formats. The same standards should apply whether the interview is conducted in person or virtually.
- **Flexibility:** Be prepared to adapt your approach based on the candidate and the interview context. Some candidates may be more comfortable in person, while others may thrive in a virtual setting.

Creating a comfortable and open environment, asking probing questions, interpreting non-verbal cues, and mastering virtual interviews are all critical components of effective interviewing. By focusing on these areas, you can navigate the complexities of modern interviewing with confidence and skill, ensuring that you can effectively assess candidates and make informed hiring decisions.

CHAPTER 4

The Interview Template

Now that we've established the importance of evaluating a candidate's viability from both the credentials and chemistry perspectives and arranged our interview setting, let's apply these ideas to the actual interview process.

Building Rapport

From the moment the interview begins, your goal is to make the candidate feel comfortable. Building rapport is key to achieving this. Start with a warm greeting and some light conversation to break the ice.

Icebreakers:

- Ask about their journey to the interview or how their day has been so far.
- Share a little about yourself or the company to create a friendly, open atmosphere.
- If the above approaches don't work, I've shared a tried-and-true technique in my template, below.

Asking Probing Questions

Probing questions are designed to delve deeper into a candidate's thought processes, experiences, and motivations. They go beyond the surface level to reveal the true capabilities and potential of the candidate.

Examples of Probing Questions:

- **Experience-Based:** "Can you describe a challenging project you worked on and how you managed it?" This question helps you understand their problem-solving skills and resilience.
- **Motivation-Based:** "What motivates you to perform at your best?" This provides insight into what drives the candidate and whether their motivations align with the company's values.
- **Behavioral:** "How do you handle conflicts within a team?" This reveals their interpersonal skills and ability to navigate

workplace dynamics.

When asking probing questions, it's crucial to listen actively and follow up on their responses with further questions. This not only shows that you are engaged but also encourages the candidate to share more.

Interpreting Non-Verbal Cues

Understanding non-verbal cues is essential in gaining a complete picture of the candidate. Body language, facial expressions, and tone of voice can all convey important information about a candidate's confidence, honesty, and engagement.

Key Non-Verbal Cues:

- **Body Language:** Open, relaxed postures indicate confidence and comfort, while crossed arms or legs may suggest defensiveness or discomfort.
- **Facial Expressions:** Smiles, nods, and consistent eye contact can signal engagement and enthusiasm. Conversely, frequent glances away or frowns might indicate uncertainty or discomfort.
- **Tone of Voice:** A steady, clear voice suggests confidence, while a shaky or hesitant tone may reveal nervousness or lack of confidence.
- **Nerves:** Often candidates are nervous, and this can be reflected in non-verbal cues. Look for such a candidate to

"warm up" as the interview proceeds.

My Personal Interview Template

Here is the template I developed in my career as an Executive Recruiter. It is specifically designed to glean as much insight into a candidate as possible within a 30-minute to 1-hour timeframe. In recruitment, you get one shot to assess the person before recommending them to a client; therefore, it's critical to interview effectively. This template served as my base interview plan and was consistently successful in helping me gain deeper insights into my candidates beyond their resumé.

I have broken down my interview template into eight sections. Each has been designed to specifically target either the credentials or chemistry facets of the candidate. Sometimes the information you're gathering is revealing on both sides of the equation, as we will see.

Here are my eight sections, along with their target area:

1. **Establish Rapport** (chemistry)
2. **Evaluate Most Recent Job Experience** (credentials)
3. **Professional History** (credentials and chemistry)
4. **The Wish List** (chemistry)
5. **Discussion of Skills and Preferences** (credentials)
6. **Discussion of Your Open Position** (credentials and chemistry)
7. **The Personal Pitch** (chemistry)
8. **The Sign-Off** (chemistry)

CHAPTER 4

The best interviews are conversational in tone and don't feel like an "interview" at all. The prompts contained in each section below are jumping-off points for conversations. You could respond to a candidate's answer with, "That's interesting, tell me more about that" in order to both cultivate a more conversational tone and learn more about a specific aspect of a candidate's background or preference.

Finally, what follows is a guideline—feel free to customize it to match your own voice.

SECTION 1: ESTABLISH RAPPORT (Chemistry)

Starting the interview can be deceptively difficult for some. If you are in need of a new approach beyond what is listed above, here's a technique I developed that worked for me every time: I would ask the candidate for their zip code. This information is rarely included on a modern resumé. Originally, this information was required for the database used by my employer, so I would ask at the start of the conversation to get it out of the way in case I would forget later. I soon realized that this was a great way to get the conversation flowing in a non-threatening and unexpected way.

This is best illustrated with an example:

"Before we begin, what's your zip code? It's required for our database and I wanted to ask before I forget." "23321." "Where is that, exactly? Richmond area?" "Yes, it's actually Carytown." "I love Carytown! What is it like living there?"

You get the idea.

SECTION 2: EVALUATE MOST RECENT JOB EXPERIENCE (Credentials)

It's tempting to get right to the most important piece of information, which is why your candidate is looking to leave the job they are in (if they are currently employed). However, there is a benefit to working up to that question by asking the candidate broad-based questions about their current role. How much they can tell you about their company is a good indicator of their level of engagement with their employer. Before asking the most obvious questions "What were your primary responsibilities in this role?" and "Why did you leave?", I take a less direct approach, asking general questions, leading into the questions about departure at the end:

- What exactly does the company do/make?
- What areas is your department responsible for?
- How is the company doing these days?
- On your resumé, you list your title as _____. What were your exact responsibilities?
- What technologies or software did you use in this role?
- Did you have any direct supervisory responsibility? If so, what were the range of titles of your direct reports?
- What was the title of your supervisor?
- Please tell me the top three ongoing responsibilities you had in this role. (For example, if I were interviewing an administrative assistant, some strong answers would be calendar management, travel/expenses facilitation, and writing/editing.)

- Why are you looking to (did you decide to) leave?

SECTION 3: PROFESSIONAL HISTORY (Credentials and Chemistry)

Now that you have established a pattern of questioning with their most recent professional experience, it's valuable to use the same prompts listed to verify the two or three roles prior to the candidate's current employment. This is also the first opportunity to explore the candidate's underlying motivations. I would add the following questions:

- You were with ABC Inc. for (length of tenure). What happened that made you decide to leave?
- If you had the opportunity to return to ABC, would you consider it? Why or why not?

In this section, I am primarily looking for the reasons behind the movement from job to job. Pay close attention to the reasons they left a role, and if the answer is vague, ask follow-up questions. These answers can provide valuable insight as to the commitment and motivations of your candidate.

SECTION 4: THE WISH LIST (Chemistry)

This is my favorite part of any interview. Now that we have validated their professional credentials, it's time to delve deeper into what makes them tick—their hopes and vision for their future. The answers are revealing and will provide you with a clearer sense of who your candidate is as a person and whether or not they might be a fit for your company. Now that we have established a connection and vetted the candidate's current work situation, it's time to broaden the conversation and uncover some of their motivations.

Introduce this next section as "the wish list" and explain that you're interested in learning more about them beyond what's on the resumé. I encourage the candidate to be candid, to think big, and have fun with these questions.

- In a perfect world, if you could design your next role for yourself, what would your next title be, and in what industry?
- Describe your ideal office environment.
- What about company culture? What would you want to see from your company?
- If there was one thing you absolutely must have in your next role, what would that be? (This could be anything: a parking spot, an office with a window, an endless supply of M&Ms at their desk).
- Is there anything you would not be willing to tolerate in your next role, and if so, what would that be? (The most common answer I'd receive was coming into the office 5 days per week).
- What is your ideal commuting situation? Of the three work

styles, please rate these from most to least preferred: hybrid, remote, in-office 5 days a week.
- What is your minimum salary requirement for making a move at this time?
- When you think about your career trajectory from this point forward, what's the one thing that motivates you the most? (Interestingly, the top answers I'd get were job security, then job status; salary was rarely mentioned first).

SECTION 5: REVIEW OF SKILLS & PREFERENCES (Credentials)

Now that I have a decent overview of the candidate's professional experience and personal motivations, I want to talk to them as a professional outside of a specific job description.

- What would you say are your top 3 professional "superpowers"? Tell me what you believe are your strongest skills. (Here, I'm looking for their personal assessment of their own skills. For an Executive Assistant, an ideal answer would be something like, "Calendar management, travel arrangements, and multitasking/working under pressure.")
- Describe how you like to be managed by your supervisor.
- Describe your own management style.
- What's your favorite aspect of being a _____?

SECTION 6: DISCUSSION OF YOUR OPEN POSITION (Credentials and Chemistry)

I've reserved this part of the interview until now because I don't want a discussion of the role being interviewed for to color the candidate's responses any more than it inevitably will. I want to establish a broader understanding of them before discussing specifics. What was learned before will enhance my understanding of their viability for the role. These questions assume the candidate has read the job description and has an idea of what the role entails.

- What's your WHY for this job?
- What will you bring to this role?
- What questions do you have regarding this position?

SECTION 7: THE PERSONAL PITCH (Chemistry)

This section is about self-possession. Everyone should be able to do an elevator pitch about themselves. My intent here is to get a sense of their self-confidence and their ability to articulate an honest, positive view of their talents and abilities. Can they authentically promote themselves and are they comfortable owning their attributes?

I would start by asking, **"What's your *sizzle*?"** If someone was able to answer immediately without asking for clarification as to what is meant by "sizzle," that was great. If clarification were needed, here are some of the questions I would follow up with:

- What's your one-up?
- What makes you a great professional?

Finally, I would close this section with this:

- What would you have me know about you that we have not touched on in our conversation so far?

SECTION 8: THE SIGN-OFF (Chemistry)

Your interview has come to an end. Clarify the next steps in the hiring process and ask the candidate if they have any further questions or needs. This final touch point ensures the candidate leaves the interview with a clear understanding of what to expect next and gives them one last opportunity to express any concerns or interests. Congratulations, you've just conducted a thorough, in-depth interview that provides you with a complete picture of your potential hire.

The structured approach of this interview template ensures that you cover all essential aspects of the candidate's profile—both credentials and chemistry. By following this guide, you can create a balanced, engaging, and insightful interview process that not only helps you make better hiring decisions but also leaves the candidate with a positive impression of your company.

Putting It All Together

For your convenience I am including the following interview "script" for your reference. This is the document I have in front of me for every interview I conduct. Again, customize to suit your personal preferences and particular requirements of whatever role(s) you are currently interviewing for.

NAME:
  ROLE APPLIED FOR:
  DATE:
  ZIP CODE:
  Notes:

CURRENT/MOST RECENT JOB EXPERIENCE:

- What exactly does the company do/make?
- What areas is your department responsible for?
- How is the company doing these days?
- On your resumé, you list your title as _____. What are/were your exact responsibilities?
- What technologies or software did you use in this role?
- Did you have any direct supervisory responsibility? If so, what are/were the range of titles of your direct reports?
- What was the title of your supervisor?
- Please tell me the top three ongoing responsibilities you have/had in this role.
- Why are you looking to (did you decide to) leave?

Notes:

PROFESSIONAL HISTORY (last two – three – roles):

- What exactly did the company do/make?
- What areas was your department responsible for?
- On your resumé, you list your title as _____. What are/were your exact responsibilities?
- What technologies or software did you use in this role?
- Did you have any direct supervisory responsibility? If so, what are/were the range of titles of your direct reports?
- What was the title of your supervisor?
- Please tell me the top three ongoing responsibilities you have/had in this role.
- You were with ABC Inc. for (length of tenure). What happened that made you decide to leave?
- If you had the opportunity to return to ABC, would you consider it? Why or why not?

Notes:

THE WISH LIST

- **In a perfect world,** if you could design your next role for yourself, what would your next title be, and in what industry?
- Describe your ideal office environment.
- What about company culture? What would you want to see from your company?

- If there was one thing you absolutely must have in your next role, what would that be?
- Is there anything you would not be willing to tolerate in your next role, and if so, what would that be?
- What is your ideal commuting situation? Of the three work styles, please rate these from most to least preferred: hybrid, remote, in-office 5 days a week.
- What is your minimum salary requirement for making a move at this time?
- When you think about your career trajectory from this point forward, what's the one thing that motivates you the most?

Notes:

DISCUSSION OF SKILLS AND PREFERENCES

- What would you say are your top 3 professional "superpowers"? Tell me what you believe are your strongest skills. Describe how you like to be managed by your supervisor.
- Describe your own preferred management style.
- What's your favorite aspect of being a _____?

Notes:

DISCUSSION OF OPEN POSITION

- What's your **WHY** for this job?
- What will you bring to this role?
- What questions do you have regarding this position?

Notes:

THE PERSONAL PITCH

- What's your professional "sizzle"?
- (follow up if needed) What's your one-up?
- (follow up if needed) What makes you a great professional?
- What would you like me to know about you that we have not touched on in our conversation so far?

Notes:

THE SIGN OFF

- Here are the next steps in this hiring process.
- Do you have any further questions for me?
- Thank you for taking the time to meet with me today!

Notes:

6

CONCLUSION

Effective interviewing is more than just filling an open position; it's about building a cohesive, dynamic team that drives your company forward. Each successful hire contributes to the culture, productivity, and overall success of your organization. By meticulously assessing both credentials and chemistry, you are setting the foundation for a thriving workplace where each employee can excel.

Building Confidence and Mastery

As you apply the techniques and strategies discussed in this book, you will notice a marked improvement in your interviewing skills. With each interview, your ability to discern the nuances of a candidate's qualifications and fit within your team will sharpen. This increased confidence will be reflected in your hiring decisions, leading to more effective and harmonious team dynamics.

Ensuring Long-Term Success

The ultimate goal of any hiring process is to bring on board individuals who will grow with the company and contribute to its long-term success. By focusing on both the professional capabilities and the personal attributes of your candidates, you are not only addressing immediate needs but also fostering a workforce that is resilient, adaptable, and aligned with your company's vision and values.

Continuous Improvement

Remember that interviewing is an evolving skill. Stay open to learning and adapting your techniques based on the feedback you receive and the outcomes you observe. The business landscape is constantly changing, and so are the dynamics of effective hiring. By remaining flexible and committed to continuous improvement, you will maintain a competitive edge in attracting and retaining top talent.

Final Thoughts

Thank you for investing your time in this book. The methodologies and insights shared are designed to equip you with a comprehensive toolkit for interviewing success. By integrating these practices into your routine, you will not only enhance your own professional growth but also contribute significantly to the success and sustainability of your organization.

In closing, I encourage you to approach each interview with curiosity, empathy, and a genuine desire to understand the person behind the resumé. This approach will not only lead to better hiring decisions but also create a more positive and respectful interview experience for your candidates. Here's to your success in building exceptional teams and fostering a thriving workplace!

7

Resources

OpenAI. ChatGPT (Editorial assistance). Version July 19, 2024, OpenAI, https://www.openai.com/.

www.ingramcontent.com/pod-product-compliance
Lightning Source LLC
Chambersburg PA
CBHW072005210526
45479CB00003B/1073